Original title:
Creative Visionaries

Author: Paul Pääsuke
ISBN HARDBACK: 978-9916-87-022-8
ISBN PAPERBACK: 978-9916-87-023-5

The Dance of Creation

In shadows deep where silence breathes,
A spark ignites, a world bequeaths.
Stars twirl in a cosmic waltz,
Unraveling threads, no need for faults.

Light and dark in sweet embrace,
Whispers echo through time and space.
Colors bloom in joyous sway,
Crafting night from the hues of day.

Celestial hands, so deftly weave,
A tapestry where dreams believe.
Mountains rise with a gentle sigh,
While rivers sing as they wander by.

Spirits dance with radiant glee,
In every heartbeat, they roam free.
Creation breathes, a lively pulse,
In every edge, a hidden impulse.

Through chaos pure, a harmony flows,
Where life awakens and courage grows.
In this dance, we all partake,
Each step a testament, a heartbeat wakes.

Portals to New Realities

Beyond the veil, a whisper calls,
Where time dissolves and shadow falls.
Glimmers shine through horizons wide,
Unseen realms where mysteries abide.

Crystalline gates, so softly gleam,
Guiding us through a waking dream.
Each threshold crossed, a story spun,
In the heart of all that's yet begun.

Echoes of laughter, soft and clear,
Resonating in a world sincere.
Fleeting visions, they come alive,
With every pulse, we learn to thrive.

In the silence, secrets bare,
Whispers of worlds beyond compare.
We are stardust, woven bright,
Time's illusion, a fleeting light.

Through portals wide, we take a chance,
To tread where dreams meet happenstance.
A new reality, vast and free,
Awaits the brave, the heart, the key.

Spark of the Imagination

In shadows deep, a flicker glows,
Ideas dance, as the spirit flows.
With every thought, a fire ignites,
Crafting worlds under starry nights.

Unseen threads weave a tale so bright,
Colors swirl, painting pure delight.
From whispered dreams, new visions soar,
Unlocking realms, we seek to explore.

An echo stirs within our chest,
A call to forge, to build, to zest.
With every spark, the heart takes flight,
A beacon shining, bold and right.

Captured moments, fleeting and rare,
Imagination blooms everywhere.
In the silence, the mind finds peace,
From chaos formed, we seek release.

With each creation, a story spun,
The journey endures, yet just begun.
Ignite your dreams, let them unfurl,
For in your heart lies a precious pearl.

Dreamweavers of Tomorrow

Through the night, our visions glide,
Weaving dreams on the cosmic tide.
With threads of hope, we intertwine,
Crafting futures, uniquely divine.

In every heart a story starts,
An echo shared, a dance of hearts.
Together we dream, together we grow,
Beneath the skies, new paths we sow.

Tomorrow calls with a gentle hand,
A canvas blank, a treasured land.
With whispers soft, the future gleams,
In the realm of countless dreams.

Each choice we make, a new thread spun,
Collective efforts yield what’s won.
With every dawn, the vision thrives,
In unity, the dream survives.

These dreamweavers chase the light,
From shadows come, to scale new heights.
In the realm where hopes collide,
Together we stand, side by side.

Architects of Inspiration

With pencil poised, we draft our dreams,
Building visions from gentle beams.
Each line a promise, a future bright,
Crafting wonders that ignite the night.

In every stroke, a heartbeat lies,
Foundations laid beneath the skies.
We blueprint hope, we sketch delight,
Transforming whispers into flight.

Inspiration flows like rivers wide,
We navigate with hearts as guide.
From thoughts untamed, to structure bold,
We shape the world, a story told.

With every dawn, new designs appear,
A testament to dreams held dear.
The architects with vision clear,
Construct the dreams we long to steer.

From fragments lost, we build anew,
A masterpiece, a vibrant hue.
With passion's fire, our spirits soar,
Creating worlds worth fighting for.

Luminaries in the Night

In the quiet dark, we shine so bright,
Guiding souls through the velvet night.
With every star, a hope revealed,
A tapestry of dreams concealed.

The cosmos sings a song of grace,
As luminaries take their place.
With every flicker, a story told,
A touch of wonder wrapped in gold.

We gather light from scattered gleams,
Illuminating faded dreams.
With open hearts, we share our spark,
Creating pathways through the dark.

In unity, our brilliance grows,
Across the sky, a love that glows.
Together we rise, casting shadows wide,
In harmony, we turn the tide.

For in the night, we find our way,
As luminous hearts guide night to day.
With every step, we blaze the trail,
In the starlit dance, we shall not fail.

Paintbrushes in the Stars

In night's embrace, we splash the void,
With colors bright, our dreams deployed.
We trace the paths of distant light,
Creating worlds that dance in night.

Galaxies swirl, a cosmic blend,
Each stroke a wish, each hue a friend.
Constellations whisper tales untold,
In brushes dipped in stardust bold.

With every twirl, the cosmos bends,
A canvas vast, where space transcends.
Infinity waits for artist's hand,
To paint the sky, a dream unplanned.

The nebulae bloom, lush and wide,
In vibrant hues, our fears collide.
A masterpiece of fate and time,
Each dot a heartbeat, each line a rhyme.

Together we soar, no bounds to see,
With paint and passion, we set hearts free.
So let us dance among the stars,
Crafting our fate, no matter how far.

Chasing Epiphanies

A glimmer breaks through cloudy minds,
Where thoughts collide, the truth unwinds.
We chase the light, a fleeting spark,
Through darkened paths, igniting the arc.

In whispered moments, visions flow,
Ideas blossom, seeds we sow.
Through trials faced, we find the gold,
In every story, wisdom behold.

Like rivers twist, our thoughts cascade,
Moments of clarity softly invade.
We grasp at straws, yet find the thread,
In bursts of insight, fears are shed.

Across the skies, we trace the signs,
Connecting dots, where destiny aligns.
Each epiphany, a guiding star,
Leading us forward, no matter how far.

In quiet dreams, our minds ignite,
Chasing the wonders that feel so right.
With open hearts, we roam the land,
Finding the pearls that life has planned.

The Rhythm of Invention

Ideas dance in electrified air,
Crafted by minds that dare to care.
Invention sings a vibrant tune,
Each note a chance, like flowers in bloom.

From quiet whispers, sparks will appear,
Creativity flows, fueled by cheer.
With open hands, we sculpt the dawn,
Transforming thoughts till the night is gone.

The clock ticks softly, but time stands still,
As we create, shaping every will.
Through trials faced, we never concede,
For in innovation, we plant the seed.

Each pulse of life, a rhythm divine,
A beat that echoes in every line.
Invention flourishes, breaking the mold,
Bold visions arise, stories unfold.

Together we dance, a collaborative grace,
In the realm of dreams, there's always a place.
With courage in heart, we seek to ignite,
The passion for progress that shines ever bright.

Builders of New Realms

With hammers raised, we carve our fate,
Crafting worlds that patiently wait.
Brick by brick, we lay the ground,
In dreams and vision, our hopes are found.

Through tunnels deep and towers high,
We chase horizons that touch the sky.
Constructing bridges where none have been,
In every heart, a spark within.

With hands of purpose, we forge anew,
Foundations strong, our spirits true.
Each tool we wield, a voice that calls,
Echoing loudly through ancient halls.

From chaos born, we shape the dawn,
Creating paths for those yet to run.
In unison, we lift our voice,
As builders of dreams, we all rejoice.

So let us dream, let us create,
In unity, the fire we sate.
For realms we build, with love and grace,
Shape destinies, and time, we embrace.

Quest for the Extraordinary

In lands where dreams dare soar high,
Beneath the vast and endless sky.
Adventurers brave, their hearts aflame,
They search for glory, seek a name.

With every step, the tales unfold,
Of ancient wisdom, treasures bold.
They navigate through shadows deep,
For in the night, lost secrets creep.

Mountains tall and rivers wide,
They face the storms, they do not hide.
With courage bright, they push on through,
In quest for what they know is true.

Each trial faced, a lesson learned,
With every page of fate they've turned.
They carve their path through thick and thin,
For in their hearts, the fire burns within.

So heed the call, O wanderer dear,
The extraordinary beckons near.
Take the leap, embrace the fight,
For in the quest, you'll find your light.

Chronicles of the Brave

Once upon a time, their tale began,
With courage held by every man.
In shadowed halls, they made their stand,
United strong, a noble band.

Through battles fierce and trials vast,
They forged their bonds and lived steadfast.
In whispers soft, their names were told,
Of valor bright and spirits bold.

With swords of justice, shields of grace,
They took the fight to every place.
For every heart that dared to dream,
They sought to mend the world's dark seam.

Each victory celebrated, each loss mourned,
With every dawn, their spirits warmed.
Together still, they rise and fall,
In chronicles of bravery, they call.

And when the night falls dark and deep,
In hearts of many, their legacy'll keep.
A tribute to those who chose to stand,
The warriors brave, a steadfast hand.

The Whisperers of Change

In quiet corners, voices swell,
Whispering truths we yearn to tell.
A gentle breeze of fresh new thought,
In every heart, a spark is caught.

From shadows cast, they seek the light,
Transforming fears and wrongs to right.
Through murmured words and subtle art,
They plant the seeds within the heart.

With every breath, they stir the air,
Invoking hope, dispelling despair.
The power found in softest tones,
Can shift the mightiest of thrones.

An echo grows, a chorus starts,
Awakening the dormant hearts.
They teach the world to stand and strive,
To feel the pulse of change alive.

So listen well, and heed the call,
For changes born in whispers small.
They ripple wide, like waves at sea,
Transforming all, including thee.

Kindling the Unimaginable

With glimmers bright, our dreams ignite,
Kindling visions, taking flight.
In realms where fantasies reside,
We spark the flames we hold inside.

Each thought a match, each wish a flame,
To chase the wild, to seek the same.
In swirling mists of endless night,
We carve new paths with sheer delight.

For magic dwells in what we seek,
In every heart, it's strong, not weak.
Through trials faced, our spirits soar,
We chase the unimaginable more.

With laughter light and joy profound,
In uncharted realms, new hopes are found.
We cling to dreams both big and small,
For in our hearts, we hold it all.

So let us gather, hearts ablaze,
Creating worlds that fill our days.
In kindling flames, we dare to dream,
Embracing all within the gleam.

In the Realm of Pioneers

In fields where dreams ignite,
They tread on paths untold,
With hope as their guiding light,
And courage to be bold.

Through whispers of the past,
Their footsteps leave a mark,
In a world built to last,
They dare to leave a spark.

With hearts that beat as one,
They carve a brighter way,
Where battles fought are won,
And night fades into day.

They dance where few have dared,
With visions clear and bright,
For every dream is shared,
In the dawn's golden light.

Together they shall rise,
In the realm of the free,
With passion in their eyes,
Creating history.

Beyond the Boundaries

Where mountains kiss the sky,
And rivers carve the earth,
They seek the question why,
In pursuit of their worth.

With wings that know no chains,
They soar on currents high,
Through laughter and through pains,
They echo a bold cry.

In lands of endless dreams,
They forge their destinies,
Crossing uncharted streams,
Unlocking mysteries.

The horizon calls them near,
With promises of change,
They cast aside all fear,
For life is vast and strange.

With every step they take,
They shape the world anew,
For every step they make,
Brings forth a brighter hue.

The Harvest of Vision

From seeds of thought they sow,
In fertile fields of mind,
With patience, love, and flow,
They nurture what's divine.

In shadows where doubt lies,
They prioritize their sights,
With open hearts that rise,
They reach for lofty heights.

The fruits of dreams abound,
In colors rich and pure,
Where knowledge can be found,
And passion shall endure.

Through labor, sweat, and tears,
They gather what they've grown,
With faith that calms all fears,
Their strength has brightly shone.

In unity they stand,
With visions intertwined,
Transforming all the land,
The harvest is defined.

Illuminating the Void

In silence where shadows creep,
They shine with inner light,
Through darkness, promises keep,
Emerging bold and bright.

With lanterns made of hope,
They navigate the night,
Through valleys wide and slope,
Their spirit takes to flight.

In every flicker shared,
They banish doubt and fear,
With whispers boldly bared,
Their vision crystal clear.

The echoes in the dark,
Resound with truth's own song,
Igniting every spark,
Reminding them they belong.

Together they shall find,
The strength to make a choice,
With hearts and hands aligned,
Illuminated voice.

Echoes of the Future

Whispers dance on time's embrace,
Fleeting shadows, unseen face.
Hopes ascend, like birds in flight,
Guiding hearts through endless night.

A world that pulses, beats anew,
Boundless skies, a vibrant hue.
Footsteps echo on the ground,
A symphony yet to be found.

Choices ripple in the stream,
Fragments of a shared dream.
Voices call from distant shores,
Telling tales of what's in store.

Foundations laid on fragile ground,
In the silence, truth is found.
Eyes that search, with purpose bright,
Illuminating hidden light.

The future sings, a hopeful song,
In every heart where dreams belong.
Echoes mingle, coalesce,
To shape a world of tenderness.

Questing for Light

Through the shadows, we will tread,
Chasing warmth where dreams are led.
Every step, a story told,
In the dark, our hearts unfold.

Glimmers shine along the way,
Guiding souls from night to day.
Courage blooms in every fight,
As we quest for vibrant light.

In the stillness, wisdom grows,
Nurtured by the path we chose.
Facing fears with love's embrace,
Unraveling the past's disgrace.

Time may bend, but spirits rise,
Painting futures in the skies.
Hope's beacon, ever bright,
Leads us forth, our souls in flight.

In this journey, bonds are forged,
Hands held tight, our dreams enlarged.
Together, we will reach the height,
In our questing for the light.

The Architect's Dream

Lines and curves in perfect grace,
Blueprints drawn in empty space.
A vision born from vivid thoughts,
In every corner, beauty caught.

Stones become the heart's desire,
Crafted dreams that never tire.
Windows open to the sky,
Framing worlds that soar and fly.

With each brick, a story's spun,
In shadows cast by setting sun.
Rooms that breathe, with colors bright,
Illuminate the canvas of night.

Echoes linger in the halls,
Memories dance as silence calls.
Every space, a tale untold,
An architect's dream to behold.

Roots of life in structures stand,
Unity in every hand.
In designs where hopes converge,
The architect's dreams emerge.

Mosaic of Perception

Fragments shine in varied light,
Serving visions, day and night.
Colors merge, each hue distinct,
In the tapestry, thoughts are linked.

Layers deep hide stories bold,
Wisdom gathered, truths unfold.
In the chaos, we can find,
Patterns woven, intertwined.

Every glance unveils the whole,
In the puzzle of the soul.
Hearts connect through shared insight,
Creating depth from purest light.

Voices rise, a symphony,
Unity in diversity.
In this blend, we start to see,
The beauty of what it means to be.

Mosaic made from love's design,
Reflections of the grand divine.
In every piece, a story’s spark,
Creating brilliance in the dark.

The Dance of Enlightenment

In shadows deep, wisdom plays,
Awakening thoughts in quiet ways.
Stars align in the silent night,
Truth spins gently, embracing light.

Each step taken, a new reveal,
In stillness, the heart starts to feel.
Dance with the whispers of the soul,
Freedom found, we become whole.

Moments twirl like leaves in air,
Sparks of insight, now laid bare.
Bridges built on the threads of fate,
In the rhythm, we resonate.

Steps echo with timeless grace,
Transcending limits of time and space.
The dance ignites the hidden flame,
In the circle, we find our name.

Join the flow, let go of doubt,
In every movement, learn to shout.
For in this dance of hope and light,
We embrace the dawn, banish night.

Colors of the Untamed Mind

Bursting forth like a painter's brush,
Fleeting thoughts in a vibrant hush.
Colors collide in a spectrum grand,
A dance of chaos, a wild stand.

From azure dreams to crimson fears,
The palette shifts through laughter and tears.
In the tapestry of thoughts that gleam,
Awake we rise, ignite the dream.

Each hue a story, each shade a tale,
Whispers of freedom, we shall not pale.
Through forests deep and rivers wide,
The colors of passion become our guide.

Fractured fragments of hidden desires,
Illuminate the heart with kindled fires.
In the garden of mind where wonders bloom,
We celebrate life, dispelling gloom.

Let the colors flow, embrace the thrill,
The mind's creation, an artist's will.
In this canvas of moments entwined,
We find our essence, the untamed mind.

Tapestry of the Bold

Woven threads of courage bright,
Stories linger in the night.
Each strand whispers tales of old,
In the fabric, the brave are told.

Hands intertwined in unity's grace,
Bold hearts dare to seek their space.
Together we stand, defying fate,
Thread by thread, we create our state.

Colors of strength, rich and deep,
In the tapestry, our dreams we keep.
Through struggles fierce, we rise anew,
Each battle fought, a richer hue.

Embroidered with laughter, stitched with pain,
In the fabric's dance, we will remain.
Bound by dreams, in harmony's hold,
We weave our saga, the tapestry bold.

Fearless souls, we take the leap,
Into the unknown, our voice we keep.
In unity's warmth, our spirits lift,
Crafting a world, a precious gift.

Invention's Serenade

Whispers of genius in the night,
Spark of creation, brilliance ignites.
Ideas swim in the mind's vast sea,
A symphony played in harmony.

The clock ticks slow, inspiration flows,
Within each thought, a wonder grows.
Papyrus scrolls and canvas bare,
Invention's song fills the air.

Crafted dreams from the heart arise,
Inventors dance beneath the skies.
With every heartbeat, new worlds unfold,
A serenade of the brave and bold.

In workshops filled with tools and light,
Glimmers shine on paths of flight.
Innovate, create, let go of fear,
As visions blur, the future's clear.

The dawn will break with hope anew,
Sing the song of the chosen few.
Invention's call, we shall obey,
Together we shape a brighter day.

Architects of Imagination

In halls where dreams take flight,
Blueprints of the starry night,
Crafting worlds with whispered grace,
Time and space a warm embrace.

With pencils drawn, our visions spark,
Sketching shadows, bright and dark,
Each creation birthed from thought,
Magic in the lines we sought.

Foundations built on hopes and fears,
Molding futures through the years,
In the silence, visions bloom,
Breaking free, dispelling gloom.

Structures formed from heart and soul,
Chasing dreams that make us whole,
In the chaos, beauty reigns,
Architects of joy and pain.

We raise our voices to the skies,
Building bridges, where truth lies,
Join the dance of mind and heart,
Crafting worlds, never to part.

Whispers of the Muse

In quiet corners, secrets dwell,
Whispers from a hidden well,
Gentle nudges, soft and clear,
Inspiration drawing near.

Brush strokes eager to embrace,
Colors mingle, find their place,
In the stillness, echoes sing,
Minds awakened by the spring.

Tender glimpses, fleeting light,
Guiding hands through darkest night,
A spark ignites, the pages turn,
In the fire, passions burn.

Every thought, a song in flight,
Taking form within the night,
As the muse begins to dance,
Crafting dreams in a trance.

Let the whispers guide the way,
In the chaos, find the sway,
With every stroke, a story's spun,
Whispers lead till day is done.

Palette of Possibilities

A canvas stretched, awaits in silence,
Colors swirl, a vibrant dance,
With each shade, a world appears,
Chasing dreams, confronting fears.

Splatters bold and lines so fine,
Mixing hues with whispered rhyme,
Creating realms both strange and wide,
In imagination, we will glide.

Every stroke a breath of fate,
In the moment, we create,
From the palette, visions rise,
Opening doors to endless skies.

Let the colors sing their tune,
Underneath the watchful moon,
With each choice, a pathway drawn,
In this dance, we will respond.

For in every shade we find,
The essence of the human mind,
A tapestry of heart and soul,
A palette that can make us whole.

Chasing the Unseen

In shadows deep, the whispers call,
Echoes dancing, never small,
Chasing hints of what could be,
Venturing into mystery.

With every step, a door we push,
Seeking truth in every hush,
Finding beauty in the rare,
Breath of magic in the air.

Fleeting moments, grains of sand,
Slipping softly through our hands,
Yet in pursuit, we find our light,
Guiding us throughout the night.

As the stars begin to gleam,
Fulfilling every latent dream,
In the chase, we come alive,
In the unseen, we will thrive.

So follow whispers, don't retreat,
In the journey lies the sweet,
Chasing visions, bold and keen,
Embracing all that lies unseen.

In the Birdcage of Thought

Behind bars of reason, we dwell,
Chasing dreams, a silent bell.
Whispers flutter like restless wings,
In this cage, imagination sings.

Thoughts collide in a vibrant dance,
Bound by logic's fleeting chance.
Yet hope breaks free in a daring flight,
Illuminating the depths of night.

Ideas bloom like fragile flowers,
Sprouting high in mental towers.
In the stillness, they search for light,
In the birdcage of endless night.

Unlocking doors with a gentle key,
The heart of the mind longs to be free.
So let each thought soar high above,
In a world crafted from dreams and love.

Within this realm where shadows play,
Awakening wonders in their own way.
In the birdcage, we learn to see,
The beauty of boundless creativity.

Bringing Shadows to Life

In the twilight, whispers sigh,
Shadows dance as day slips by.
Shapes emerge from the dusk’s embrace,
Bringing stories to every space.

Figures flicker on the wall,
Echoes of life that dare to call.
With each stroke of the fading light,
We breathe warmth into the night.

A canvas made of dreams and fears,
Painting visions with silent tears.
Through the shadows, we chase the bright,
Finding depth within the night.

Every heartbeat sings a tune,
Merging dreams with the silver moon.
In the dance of dark and light,
We find our truth, a guiding sight.

Bringing shadows to life anew,
Awakening magic, old and true.
In each flicker, a story we weave,
In the shadows, we learn to believe.

Maps of Innate Potential

Beneath the surface, treasures gleam,
Hidden maps guide our dream.
Each line drawn tells a tale,
Of journeys where we dare not pale.

In valleys deep, in mountains high,
Potential rests beneath the sky.
With every step, we chart the course,
To unlock the inner force.

Lines of fate in the sand we trace,
Winding paths to a sacred place.
Within our hearts, the compass spins,
Revealing wonders where life begins.

Lost in the maze, yet never alone,
With every twist, the seeds we've sown.
Mapping hopes with devoted care,
To uncover the dreams we dare.

In the tapestry of time, we find,
The threads of fate intricately bind.
Maps of potential, drawn with love,
Guiding each star in the sky above.

The Journey of Invention

In the mind’s eye, sparks ignite,
Flickering flames in the still of night.
Ideas born in a gentle sigh,
The journey begins with a curious why.

Through trials tough, we persist and mold,
Crafting futures from visions bold.
In every stumble, lessons bloom,
Transforming chaos into the room.

Blueprints sketched in the light of dawn,
Turning whispers into a song.
With each creation, the world expands,
A story written by eager hands.

Fusing thoughts with passion's embrace,
Finding magic in every space.
The journey of invention, a sacred quest,
To fashion wonders beyond the rest.

As dreams take flight, horizons bend,
We chase the light around each bend.
In the heart of creation, we find our way,
The journey of invention, come what may.

Vanguards of Vision

A spark ignites the night,
Courage breeds in minds so bright.
With dreams that soar, we take our flight,
Vanguards of change, we embrace the fight.

Through shadows deep, our voices rise,
A chorus built on truth and wise.
We weave a tale beneath the skies,
Lighting paths where hope defies.

Each step we take, foundations laid,
In unity, our fears allayed.
Together strong, we'll not be swayed,
In every heart, our dreams portrayed.

The future calls, we dare to chase,
With visions bold, we set our pace.
Exploring realms, transcending space,
In every heart, we find our place.

An echo of the past resounds,
A legacy in hope abounds.
For every heart that courage found,
In vanguards strong, the road unwound.

The Alchemy of Ideas

From whispers soft, concepts bloom,
Shaping visions in the gloom.
With minds that dance, we find our room,
The alchemy of thoughts dispels the doom.

Ideas blend like colors bright,
Creating worlds that spark delight.
In unity, they take their flight,
Transforming darkness into light.

We forge the new from dreams we mold,
Each story shared, a truth unfolds.
In every idea, a treasure holds,
A tapestry of hearts retold.

Through trials fierce, we test our fire,
In every spark, a new desire.
With passion's heat, we lift us higher,
The alchemy of dreams inspires.

Let every thought, with purpose gleam,
In collaboration, we dare to dream.
Together we'll ignite the stream,
The alchemy of vision, our shared theme.

Stepping into the Unknown

With trembling hearts, we take the leap,
Into the dark, the vast and deep.
Embracing change, our fears we keep,
Stepping forth, our dreams will seep.

In every doubt, a lesson learned,
The fire of courage fiercely burned.
With open minds, the tides are turned,
In pathways new, our spirits yearned.

The horizon calls, with whispers light,
Guiding us through the shadowed night.
Each step we take, igniting sight,
In unknown realms, we find our might.

As chapters close, new tales begin,
In every loss, a chance to win.
With every heart, we dive within,
Stepping forth, our lives entwined.

With courage strong, we seek and find,
The mysteries that fate aligned.
In stepping out, the truth defined,
Together bold, our spirits bind.

Beyond the Canvas

Brush strokes dance with vibrant hue,
Crafting stories, both old and new.
A silent voice that speaks so true,
Beyond the canvas, visions grew.

Colors clash in wild array,
In emotion's lap, they gently sway.
Each painting tells what words can't say,
Beyond the canvas, dreams will play.

With layers deep, we reveal our soul,
In every piece, a journey whole.
The artist's heart, a sacred scroll,
Beyond the canvas, we feel the whole.

In shadows cast, our truths are shown,
In light's embrace, we’ve brightly grown.
The beauty lies in seeds we've sown,
Beyond the canvas, love is known.

Each artwork breathes, a life behind,
An invitation to those aligned.
Discover worlds, both vast and kind,
Beyond the canvas, we’re intertwined.

Odyssey of the Dreamweavers

In the realm of whispers, dreams take flight,
Weaving threads of silver, through the night.
Stars guide the journey, bright and clear,
With every heartbeat, the dreamers steer.

In valleys of thought, where fantasies play,
Colors dance freely, blending night and day.
Boundless horizons call out their name,
In a tapestry woven, igniting the flame.

Through portals unseen, they wander and roam,
Crafting their visions, they find their home.
Each step a story, a fate intertwined,
With the pulse of the universe, they are aligned.

In laughter and sorrow, the weavers unite,
Over mountains of doubt, into the light.
Their odyssey whispers, the secrets they hold,
In each fleeting moment, eternity unfolds.

Fragments of Infinity

Scattered like stardust, glimmers of time,
Moments entwined in an endless rhyme.
Each heartbeat echoes, a whisper so grand,
Cascading through ages, like grains of sand.

In shadows and light, the stories reside,
In the silence of night, secrets abide.
Fragments of laughter, of joy and of tears,
Mosaic of memories spanning the years.

Through the timeworn paths of wisdom and youth,
We gather the pieces, searching for truth.
In every reflection, a mirror appears,
Images flicker, dissolving our fears.

Infinite echoes, forever they soar,
Carving their presence on destiny's shore.
In the space between dreams, they softly ignite,
Fragments of infinity, merging with light.

The Alchemy of Ideas

In the cauldron of thought, ideas arise,
Fleeting and fragile, like whispers in skies.
With a spark of intention, they twist and they turn,
Alchemy brewing, a passion to burn.

Crafting the visions with clarity pure,
Transforming the mundane, seeking a cure.
Each notion a whisper, a seed in the soil,
Nurtured by dreams, they flourish with toil.

Through the lens of the mind, the magic unfolds,
Turning the abstract to treasures of gold.
Curiosity dances, igniting the flame,
Within every heartbeat, the alchemical name.

Ideas like constellations embolden the night,
Bringing forth clarity, bathing in light.
In the dance of creation, synergy sings,
The alchemy blossoms, a tapestry of things.

Beyond the Ordinary

In the stillness of dawn, a whisper is heard,
Promising wonders, as dreams take their word.
Beyond the horizon, where silence can sing,
Awake to the magic that each moment brings.

Through a veil of the mundane, we often must see,
The beauty that beckons, sets our spirits free.
In shadows of doubt, let courage ignite,
For realms unexplored, found just out of sight.

With hearts wide open, we venture afar,
Stepping beyond what we think that we are.
Each heartbeat a canvas, each breath a new start,
In the tapestry woven, we play our part.

Embrace the unknown, let passion be keen,
In the dance of existence, the spaces between.
Beyond the ordinary, life starts to gleam,
Awakening wonders, igniting the dream.

Voices from the Abyss of Ideas

Whispers echo deep within,
Shadows dance in silent thought,
Lost in realms of unformed dreams,
Ideas flicker, never caught.

Eclipsing doubts that cloud the way,
A spark ignites the unknown path,
Boldly diving into the fray,
With fervor that defies the math.

Visions rise like spectral flames,
Challenging the weary mind,
Each voice a note in life's great games,
A harmony that's yet to find.

Riddles wrapped in twilight's veil,
Each whisper a call to the brave,
Daring hearts will not let fail,
In the depths, new worlds they pave.

From shadows born, they fight and soar,
Crimson trails in vast expanse,
In the abyss, we search for more,
With every risk, the chance to dance.

The Essence of Enchantment

In twilight's glow, the world transforms,
Magic flutters on the breeze,
Glimmers wrapped in quiet forms,
A wish appears among the trees.

Petals whisper secrets sweet,
Underneath the silver moon,
With every step, heart skips a beat,
To nature’s soft and soothing tune.

Stars align in mystic play,
Their light a guide through shadowed halls,
Casting dreams on distant clay,
Where every echo softly calls.

In the depths of silence found,
Imagination takes its flight,
New realms bloom upon the ground,
Enchanting whispers through the night.

Hold the wonder, don’t let go,
Embrace the magic of the now,
Let it flourish, let it grow,
For enchantment lives in every vow.

Threads of New Horizons

Spun from dreams, the threads unwind,
Woven paths in vibrant hues,
Crossing borders of the mind,
With every stitch, the old renews.

A journey starts with a single thread,
Through valleys deep and mountains high,
In every step, the heart is led,
To find the beauty, to touch the sky.

Horizons shift like morning light,
Colors blend in soft embrace,
Each moment crafted, pure delight,
A tapestry we dare to trace.

Hands entwined, we forge ahead,
With courage born from shared design,
In every word, a promise said,
To weave our fate, to brightly shine.

Together we create the map,
With threads unbroken, strong, and true,
In this dance of life, no gap,
For new horizons wait for you.

Unleashing the Mind’s Eye

Awakening the dormant dreams,
Visions swirling, brightly set,
Beyond the veil, where hope redeems,
A realm where no regret is met.

Through corridors of endless thought,
Ideas burst like stars at night,
Each concept, fiercely, dearly sought,
Unleashing realms, igniting light.

See the world with open heart,
Beyond the canvas, past the pain,
In every detail, we create art,
With colors rich like summer rain.

Break the chains that hold you fast,
Let insight flow like rivers wide,
In the expanse of futures cast,
Be fearless, let your spirit glide.

The mind's eye is a magic key,
To unlock dreams that brightly soar,
With every glance, embrace the free,
For within lies an endless door.

The Uncharted Imagination

In the realm where dreams collide,
Visions swirl, like ghosts that ride.
Colors dance in whispered tones,
Unseen paths to distant thrones.

Each thought a spark, a fleeting light,
Guiding us through endless night.
Waves of wonder wash the shore,
Open doors to worlds explore.

Echoes resonate with grace,
Chasing shadows, we embrace.
Curiosity leads the way,
To uncharted lands we sway.

In silence, stories weave and spin,
With every loss, we find a win.
A tapestry of hopes unfurled,
Crafting our own secret world.

So let the mind's eye take its flight,
Across horizons, bold and bright.
For in the heart of imagination,
Lies the seed of creation's foundation.

Lumens of the Enlightened

Glistening beams that pierce the veil,
Wisdom’s whispers in the gale.
Illuminated by the truth,
Guiding souls, restoring youth.

From shadows deep, the light escapes,
Illuminating dreams that drape.
Every thought a shimmering glow,
In this radiant world we sow.

Questions bloom like flowers rare,
In enlightened hearts, we dare.
Seek the answers, find the way,
Let the dawn break through the gray.

In congregation of the wise,
Collective visions arise.
Through the darkness, hope ignites,
Carrying us to dizzy heights.

A journey guided by the spark,
Each lumens brightens up the dark.
For in the light, we come to see,
The endless paths to harmony.

Lighthouses of Thought

Upon the shore, they stand so tall,
Guardians guiding one and all.
Bearing wisdom from far and wide,
In their glow, dreams cannot hide.

With every wave, their beams extend,
Navigating us around the bend.
A lighthouse calls through fog and night,
To center minds in radiant light.

Thoughts like ships, they drift and roam,
Searching for a place called home.
Each beacon shines a path defined,
Illuminating the seeking mind.

In storms of doubt, their strength we seek,
A guiding voice when spirits weak.
They stand as symbols, firm and clear,
In ports of clarity, we steer.

So let your thoughts be like the waves,
In lighthouses, find what saves.
For in the light of shared insight,
We rise together, hearts in flight.

The Sculptors of Reality

With every chisel, dreams are carved,
In stone and time, we are starved.
Shaping fate with steady hands,
Forging life in grand designs.

Visions form beneath the dust,
In each creation, hope and trust.
They mold the clay of day to day,
Creating worlds in their own way.

Crafting tales that breathe and live,
In art, we learn how to forgive.
Every stroke, a piece of soul,
In the journey, we find our role.

Reality bends to the design,
Of those who dare to cross the line.
With heart and mind, they set the stage,
Turning life from grey to sage.

So let us sculpt with every breath,
Creating beauty, defying death.
For in our hands, the power lies,
To shape the world and touch the skies.

The Art of Becoming

In the silence of night, we grow,
Whispers of dreams begin to flow.
Each step a brushstroke, bold and bright,
Crafting our futures out of the night.

With every choice, a path revealed,
In the canvas of life, our hearts are healed.
Colors blend and shadows play,
In the art of becoming, we find our way.

Fears like ghosts may linger near,
Yet courage blooms, we persevere.
With hands that shape and minds that soar,
Each moment a treasure, forevermore.

Embrace the change that warms the soul,
In the dance of becoming, we are whole.
Like rivers that twist and mountains that rise,
We unfold ourselves under open skies.

Becoming is a journey, not a race,
In every heartbeat, we find our place.
So paint with passion, let your spirit be free,
In the grand masterpiece of “me”.

A Symphony of Thoughts

In the orchestra of the mind, we play,
Each note a whisper of the day.
Melodies rise, like hopes in flight,
A symphony unfolds in the quiet night.

Harmony dances through darkest fears,
Resonating truths through laughter and tears.
In every silence, a cadence grows,
As the heartbeats pulse, the music flows.

Fragments of ideas, a rhythmic stream,
Weaving connections, chasing a dream.
In the space between breath and sigh,
A symphony of thoughts begins to fly.

Echoes linger in spaces wide,
Complications fade as we turn the tide.
With every chord, our spirits entwine,
In this vast concert, we brightly shine.

Listen closely, let your heart guide,
In this symphony, let love abide.
For every moment holds a song,
In the melody of life, we all belong.

Threads of the Unknown

Woven in shadows, threads unfold,
Mysteries whispered, stories untold.
Each step we take, a venture bold,
In the fabric of time, a treasure we hold.

The unknown beckons with gentle grace,
Lost in the maze, we find our place.
Stitched with wonder, adorned with dreams,
In the tapestry of life, nothing is as it seems.

Fingers entwined with destiny's thread,
Mapping the paths where angels tread.
Adventure calls with a voice so sweet,
In the dance of life, adventure we meet.

Through fog and doubt, our spirits rise,
Navigating realms with open eyes.
For every thread, a bond is spun,
In the journey forward, we have just begun.

With courage woven into our seams,
We wear the fabric of our dreams.
In the threads of the unknown, we find our song,
A tapestry of courage where we all belong.

Mosaics of Potential

In pieces scattered, we begin to see,
Mosaics of potential yearning to be free.
Each shard a story, a fragment of light,
Together they shimmer, brilliant and bright.

Colors collide in a beautiful way,
Crafting a vision where hope can sway.
With hands that gather and hearts that mold,
We create a future, vibrant and bold.

Tiny moments become the whole,
A tapestry rich, it starts to unroll.
In every crack, a chance to grow,
Mosaics of potential continue to flow.

Embrace the chaos, let it inspire,
A collage of dreams that never tire.
For in our fragments, we find our worth,
In the mosaics of potential, we celebrate birth.

Look closely now, see what you find,
Beauty in pieces, no need to rewind.
In each tiny moment, our spirits engage,
In the art of becoming, we turn the page.

Echoes of Inspiration

In the quiet dawn of day,
Whispers of dreams at play,
Ideas dance like morning light,
Kindling hope, setting hearts bright.

Through shadows deep, they flow,
Each moment crafted, to grow,
Voices soft, yet so profound,
In every heartbeat, they're found.

With every step, we rise anew,
Facing challenges we pursue,
In the echoes, strength we find,
A tapestry of the mind.

Lifting spirits high above,
Sewn together with threads of love,
Creating paths where none had been,
In the silence, we are seen.

Let inspiration guide the way,
In every moment, every sway,
For in this dance, we understand,
The power lies within our hands.

Visionaries on the Horizon

On the edge of time we stand,
With visions dreamt, like grains of sand,
Eyes aflame with sparks of light,
Charting courses, taking flight.

Each thought a beacon, shining clear,
Unfolding futures we hold dear,
With every heartbeat, new ideas flow,
Taking steps where few would go.

In the tapestry of deep-blue skies,
Lies the essence of our tries,
Cultivating seeds of what could be,
With courage and audacity.

They rise like stars from distant shores,
Daring to dream, daring to explore,
Together we weave a brighter tale,
In unity, we will not fail.

Through storms of doubt and fears unseen,
We stand as one, crafty and keen,
With visions bold, we dare to dream,
Creating a world where all may gleam.

Starlit Pathways

Under the blanket of a velvet night,
Starlit pathways shimmer bright,
Guiding souls through shadows cast,
Whispers of wonders unsurpassed.

With every step, the cosmos sings,
Sparks of joy, the night brings,
In the quiet, hearts ignite,
Dancing shadows, pure delight.

We walk among the gleaming light,
Tracing dreams in the cool twilight,
The universe speaks in silent ways,
Inviting us to weave our plays.

Footprints marked in the cosmic dust,
Gathering dreams, in hope we trust,
Each star a story to unfold,
In the darkness, courage bold.

Let the night unveil its grace,
In starlit pathways, find our place,
For as we wander, we shall see,
The beauty in our shared journey.

Constellations of Thought

In the realm of thought we dwell,
Where ideas blossom and swell,
Constellations forming bright,
Guiding minds with pure insight.

Each moment a spark ignites,
Connecting paths through endless nights,
In the vast expanse of our dreams,
Every thread together seams.

Thoughts like stars, they overlap,
Creating patterns, a cosmic map,
In the silence, wisdom blooms,
Filling the shadows, brightening rooms.

Embracing visions, wide and free,
In the universe, we find the key,
As constellations guide our way,
Never knowing what they may say.

So let us gather, minds unite,
In the glow of the celestial night,
For in our thoughts, the world expands,
Crafting futures with gentle hands.

Shaping the Ethereal

In twilight's glow, shadows play,
With whispers soft, the night turns gray.
Dreams drift like leaves on gentle winds,
Time reveals where the journey begins.

Stars awaken in the silent dark,
Guiding lost souls with their spark.
Each moment a breath, a chance to be,
Molding the realms of eternity.

In the tapestry woven from light,
Threads of color shine so bright.
Mysteries beckon with every glance,
Inviting the heart to dare and dance.

In the echo of the moon's soft hum,
Visions arise, the dreams become.
The canvas stretches across the skies,
As art transcends where spirit flies.

With each heartbeat, creation swells,
In harmony, the essence dwells.
Shaping the ethereal, hand in hand,
Together we weave, forever we'll stand.

The Pulse of Originality

In the core of every soul,
Lies a rhythm, a unique role.
Echoes of heartbeats, loud and clear,
Crafting stories from what we fear.

Colors burst in wild display,
Painting feelings in grand array.
No two strokes are ever the same,
Boldly dancing in the flame.

A whisper floats on the cool night air,
The pulse of dreams, beyond compare.
Chasing shadows that dare to flee,
Awakening the truth in me.

In the quiet, creativity calls,
Not afraid of the rise or falls.
Every heartbeat, a truth unveiled,
A journey where the brave have sailed.

With courage as the guiding light,
We carve our mark, we reach new height.
Originality flows and streams,
In the tapestry of our dreams.

Celestial Storytellers

Underneath the cosmic dome,
Stars whisper tales of far-off home.
Galaxies spin in ancient dance,
Each flicker a chance, a fleeting glance.

Comets sketch paths across the night,
With luminous trails, they ignite delight.
Voices of the universe merge,
In harmony, the wonders surge.

Nebulas cradle new worlds in birth,
Painting the vastness of cosmic mirth.
Every star, a pulse, a silent bard,
In the depth of night, their truth unmarred.

As moons weave stories in silver thread,
Echoes of myths, unspoken yet said.
Celestial storytellers in flight,
Carving the essence of infinite light.

So listen closely as dusk unfolds,
The universe breathes in the stories told.
In every twinkle and cosmic sigh,
We find our place in the vast sky.

Languages of the Heart

In the silence, emotions speak,
A gentle touch, the bond we seek.
Each glance tells tales of how we feel,
In the space where the hearts can heal.

Words unspoken, yet understood,
In soft gestures, the love is good.
Every heartbeat a language unique,
Painting the world, our spirits speak.

Through laughter shared and tears that fall,
We connect deeply, answering the call.
In the rhythm of closeness, we find our way,
Navigating the night, welcoming the day.

In quiet moments or joyful cheer,
Languages weave when souls draw near.
Expressions dance like leaves in the breeze,
Binding our hearts with delicate ease.

Together we build a world so bright,
In the languages of love, we ignite.
With each heartbeat, a story unfurls,
Uniting the threads of our vast worlds.

The Chronicle of Pioneering Spirits

In the quiet dawn, they rise anew,
Hearts ablaze with purpose, bold and true.
Paths untraveled, yet they dare to roam,
They carve their futures, making dreams their home.

With hands of strength, they build from dust,
Facing the tempest, in hope they trust.
Voices unite in a resolute song,
Together they forge where they all belong.

Through valleys low and mountains high,
Bound by a vision that will not die.
Each step a story, each moment a fight,
Their legacy glows in the tapestry bright.

With wisdom passed through ages of yore,
They stand on shoulders, reaching for more.
Echoes of courage shape the air,
Inspiring hearts, igniting the flare.

Through storms they wander, yet never wane,
Adventurers seeking, never in vain.
They chart the stars, a luminous trail,
Pioneering spirits that will not fail.

Tides of Transformation

The ocean whispers, waves collide,
Change is coming, the currents guide.
From calm to chaos, the dance unfolds,
Stories of growth in the depths untold.

In the ebb and flow, we learn to bend,
Shifting like sand, we find our end.
Emerging stronger, like the tide's embrace,
We rise renewed, reclaiming our place.

Seas of uncertainty, brave hearts set sail,
Navigating storms with courage prevail.
Each crest and trough teaches us grace,
In the heart of the tide, we find our pace.

As night meets day, and shadows flee,
Transformation blooms like a wild sea.
With every wave, the old must yield,
For in letting go, new dreams are revealed.

Through the cycles of life, we ebb and flow,
Wherever we wander, let our spirits glow.
In the tides of change, together we thrive,
For in every ending, new hopes arrive.

The Call of the Visionaries

Whispers in the dark, a voice so clear,
Visionaries rise, casting out fear.
With eyes on the future, they pave the way,
Dreams like arrows, guiding the day.

From shadows of doubt, their light breaks through,
Sketching possibilities, fresh as dew.
Innovators gather, hearts intertwined,
A chorus of brilliance, a force redefined.

With courage to dream, they stand as one,
Creating a world where hope can run.
Ideas take flight on luminous wings,
In the hands of visionaries, magic springs.

Through challenges faced, they find their might,
Turning the darkness to dazzling light.
Each spark ignites a revolutionary dance,
Together they rise, a bold second chance.

Elders of thought, guiding the young,
In every heartbeat, the future is sung.
The call of the bold rings loud and true,
In the hearts of the visionaries, dreams break through.

Stars Born from Ideas

In the canvas of night, ideas ignite,
Tiny sparks flicker, casting their light.
From whispers of thought, constellations grow,
Stars born of dreams, in the cosmos aglow.

Each concept a beacon, shimmering bright,
Illuminating paths through the shadowed night.
Creativity pulses in the cosmic expanse,
Where visions emerge in a shimmering dance.

With careful intention, we weave our dreams,
In the universe vast, nothing's as it seems.
The birth of a star brings tales to be told,
Of hopes that remain, both daring and bold.

From the depths of our minds, new worlds arise,
Carried on whispers, floating through skies.
Ideas entwined like a celestial vine,
In the hearts of dreamers, the stars brightly shine.

So let us create, with wonderous grace,
Every thought a spark in this boundless space.
For within us all, a universe thrives,
Stars born from ideas, the cosmos alive.

Threads of Connection

In soft whispers, we share our dreams,
Each thread woven, bursting at the seams.
A tapestry rich, in colors so bright,
Binding us close, like day into night.

Through laughter and tears, we find our way,
With every moment, together we stay.
Connections unbroken, though distance may call,
In this vast world, we stand strong, never small.

Memories linger, like stars in the sky,
Bright beacons of hope, they never deny.
In silence or noise, we find common ground,
In the web of our hearts, true love will abound.

Hands held together, we journey afar,
Each step a reminder, just who we are.
Through valleys and peaks, we'll venture, hand in hand,
Creating a future, together we stand.

So let us weave gently, each life as a thread,
In the quilt of existence, where all fears are shed.
For in every connection, beneath the vast sky,
We find our belonging, together we fly.

The Dance of Ideas

In a circle of thoughts, ideas take flight,
Whirling around, they ignite the night.
Each spark a potential, waiting to shine,
A dance of creation, where souls intertwine.

In flickers of brilliance, we sway to the tune,
Unraveling whispers, beneath the full moon.
With rhythm of passion, innovation unfolds,
The canvas of minds, a story retold.

As shadows grow long, and dreams intertwine,
We give life to visions, both yours and mine.
Layer by layer, we brush and we blend,
Each stroke of genius, we fervently send.

The pulse of our dreams beats in harmony's way,
A ballet of thoughts, that forever will stay.
In this jubilant dance, we'll twirl and we'll glide,
With open arms wide, we embrace what resides.

So let us take flight on this canvas of air,
Where ideas converge, become treasures we share.
For in every heartbeat, creativity thrives,
In the dance of ideas, we feel most alive.

Visionaries in Bloom

In gardens of thought, ideas do sprout,
Visionaries rise, breaking free from doubt.
With petals of wisdom, they reach for the sky,
A promise of growth, as seasons pass by.

From whispers of hope, to the loudest acclaim,
These seeds of tomorrow, we nurture the same.
With sunlight of passion, and rain of belief,
In every small moment, we find our relief.

As blossoms unfold, like dreams in the morn,
Each vision ignites, a new world is born.
With roots intertwined, we reach out to share,
Creating a future that's vibrant and rare.

Through the storms we weather, together we stand,
Cultivating strength, as we hold each hand.
In unity's embrace, we rise and we bloom,
For all of our dreams chase away the gloom.

So let us be brave, and dream without fear,
With vision and purpose, our path will be clear.
In gardens of growth, where all hearts can see,
Together we flourish, forever we'll be.

Navigating the Dreamscape

In the vast expanse where visions soar high,
We wander through dreams, let our spirits fly.
Through layers of colors, and echoes of light,
We dance on the edges of magic and night.

With every new step, the horizon unfolds,
Guided by hope, all the tales to be told.
In the whispers of silence, clarity glows,
As we follow the threads where imagination flows.

Each heartbeat a compass, in search of our truth,
Awakening wonder, reclaiming our youth.
In this dreamscape, we chase and explore,
Boundless adventures, with so much in store.

Through valleys of doubt, and mountains of grace,
We navigate currents that time can't erase.
With courage our vessel, we sail through the storm,
In the ocean of dreams, our spirits transform.

So let us embark on this journey unknown,
With all of our hearts, and courage we've grown.
For in navigating dreams, our destiny gleams,
In the tapestry woven from the fabric of dreams.

The Rebel's Palette

Colors clash in wild embrace,
Scarlet thoughts, a bold trace.
Raging hues of freedom call,
In this chaos, I stand tall.

Brushes dance with careless grace,
Canvas holds my fierce face.
Stormy skies and vibrant dreams,
Every stroke, a rebellion screams.

Whispers shun the quiet night,
Fractured shapes in stark daylight.
Palette spills like tales untold,
Rebel spirit, fierce and bold.

Through the colors, shadows play,
Echoes of a brighter day.
In rebellion, find my art,
A painted path, a beating heart.

With each layer, walls collapse,
Fading lines, dissolving traps.
In the chaos, I am free,
Crafting worlds that dare to be.

Fabulations of the Heart

Whispers woven through the air,
Tender tales of love and care.
Each flutter speaks of dreams anew,
In the silence, feelings grew.

Stories dance on pages bare,
Fables spun from deep despair.
Yet, hope glimmers in the dark,
In every line, a tiny spark.

Echoes of a heartfelt sigh,
Capturing moments, what goes by.
The warmth of laughter, tears that flow,
In every pulse, emotions grow.

Ink drips down like melting gold,
Crafting secrets, soft and bold.
Between the verses, hearts entwine,
In these fabulations, we align.

Through the rhythm, love will guide,
With every word, we will abide.
In spins and turns, stories soar,
Fabulations, forevermore.

The Inspire of Things Unseen

Veils of mist conceal the light,
Invisible threads twist through the night.
In shadows lie the truths we seek,
Whispers carried, soft yet sleek.

Glimmers flicker in the dark,
Silent wonders leave their mark.
Beyond the veil, existence hums,
In silence, hopeful promise drums.

The unseen flows through every breath,
Life's vibrant pulse beyond the death.
In quiet corners, beauty hides,
In every heartbeat, spirit guides.

Echoes linger in the still,
Fleeting moments stir the will.
Through the unseen, we create,
A universe we elevate.

Inspire found in what's obscure,
In mysteries, our hearts are sure.
Through the silence, we confide,
The unseen worlds, our hearts reside.

Beyond the Canvas

Layers deep, the stories told,
Verses trapped in colors bold.
Brushstrokes whisper secrets shared,
On this canvas, dreams laid bare.

Beyond the edge, the world expands,
Where imagination gently stands.
In every outline, magic flows,
In the stillness, the artist knows.

Through the frame, a vision swells,
In this space, my spirit dwells.
Beyond the canvas, journeys start,
Crafting realms that touch the heart.

In colors bright, potential stirs,
The canvas breathes as silence purrs.
Every image, a story spun,
In this world, we all are one.

Beyond the canvas, horizons gleam,
Painting life, a vivid dream.
In strokes of fate, we intertwine,
Beyond the canvas, love aligns.

The Allure of the Abstract

In shades of dusk, a canvas glows,
Whispers of dreams, where thought flows.
Shapes twist and meld in vibrant light,
Each stroke a secret, hidden from sight.

Mysteries dance in patterns rare,
Colors intertwine with delicate care.
Lines break the rules, they twist and weave,
In the abstract realm, we dare to believe.

Emotion swirls in every hue,
A silent song, a world anew.
Visions collide, the heart takes flight,
In the allure of the abstract night.

Fragments of truth, they flicker and spark,
In this gallery deep, we wander the dark.
Every piece tells a story untold,
A tapestry of feelings, vivid and bold.

So let us linger, lose track of time,
In the abstract world, where reason can't climb.
For within each shape, a universe gleams,
An invitation to wander through dreams.

Mosaic of the Mind’s Eye

Scattered pieces, a vivid design,
A patchwork of thoughts, all yours and mine.
Tile by tile, the story is spun,
In the mosaic, we find our fun.

Bright shards of laughter, whispers of pain,
Colors that shimmer, moments that wane.
Each fragment a journey, a place in our soul,
Together they form a beautiful whole.

In the chaos, there’s beauty we find,
A reflection of the heart and the mind.
Wonders revealed as each layer is laid,
In the mosaic, our truths are portrayed.

With each step closer, the picture gets clear,
Lessons and memories, joys, and fear.
A dance of reflections, forever in flow,
In the mind's eye, we continue to grow.

So cherish the pieces, the colors, the light,
In this intricate dance, we take flight.
Mosaic of life, so rich and divine,
In every small shard, a connection we find.

Charting the Intangible

Invisible threads weave through the air,
Mapping the emotions, deep and rare.
Paths of connection, unseen yet felt,
In the whispers of silence, secrets are dealt.

A glimmer of hope in the shadow's embrace,
In the heart’s quiet chambers, we find our place.
The intangible beckons, with secrets to show,
In the depths of the soul, like rivers that flow.

In the realm of belief, we chart our course,
Riding the currents, we tap into force.
Though invisible, it unfurls its might,
Guiding our spirits, illuminating the night.

Collective dreams share a cosmic space,
Each thought a ripple in infinite grace.
Through the fog of spirit, we navigate wide,
Charting the intangible, our hearts as our guide.

So let us embark on this wondrous quest,
Embracing the unseen, where spirits can rest.
For in every breath, lies a story profound,
Charting the intangible, our truth to be found.

Whirlwind of Inspiration

A tempest brews, a spark ignites,
Ideas swirl like dancing lights.
Whispers of muses call from afar,
In the whirlwind's embrace, we find who we are.

Thoughts take flight on the breeze of chance,
Each notion a step in a spontaneous dance.
With every turn, creativity flows,
In the whirlwind of inspiration, the passion grows.

Moments collide, a symphony plays,
A melody woven through countless arrays.
In chaos and order, we reach for the stars,
Inspiration's current, no matter how far.

Every gust brings a chance to explore,
Unlocking the doors to imagination's core.
Soaring high on wings of belief,
In the whirlwind, we find our relief.

Let us surrender to this swirling delight,
Embrace the unknown, bask in the light.
For in the whirlwind, our spirits take flight,
In the heart of creation, we shine ever bright.

The Conductor's Symphony

In shadows of the night, he stands tall,
A baton raised high, ready to call.
Strings whisper softly, the brass play bold,
The story unfolds in harmonies told.

Each note a heartbeat, in sync with the stars,
Melodies dance, erasing our scars.
The orchestra blooms, a tapestry bright,
Guided by passion, igniting the night.

The audience sways, their spirits take flight,
Lost in the magic, bathed in the light.
With every crescendo, emotions arise,
Creating a world that mesmerizes.

A whisper of silence, then thunderous cheer,
He bows with a smile, the end drawing near.
In the echoes of sound, a moment preserved,
A symphony woven, forever observed.

A legacy born on the wings of the notes,
In hearts and in minds, the music promotes.
Each concert a journey, each song a fresh start,
The conductor's vision, a work of pure art.

Mosaic of Dreams

A canvas of colors, stories entwined,
Each piece a whisper, a glimpse of the mind.
Fragments of hopes, both shattered and whole,
Painting a journey deep in the soul.

Shimmering visions, in twilight's embrace,
Every shard tells a tale, a memory's trace.
Bright futures await, in patterns so clear,
Held close to the heart, our dreams we revere.

The mountains rise high, against oceans blue,
An artist's ambition, forever in view.
Together in chaos, yet somehow aligned,
The mosaic of dreams, uniquely designed.

Threads of our struggles, in sunlight they gleam,
Reflections of courage, inspiring our team.
We gather in circles, our spirits combine,
In this vibrant mosaic, our visions align.

Each piece is a promise, a wish, a delight,
With every new layer, we reach for the light.
Through laughter and tears, our masterpiece grows,
A tapestry woven from dreams that we chose.

Seeds of Inspiration

Planted in silence, deep in the earth,
Tiny intentions await their birth.
Nurtured by sunlight, kissed by the rain,
Sprouting with passion, their purpose is plain.

Whispers of hope in the soft morning breeze,
Encouraging growth with the rustling leaves.
From the darkest corners, they push into light,
Transformative power, an inspiring sight.

Buds open gently, emissions of dreams,
Unfurling their beauty in vibrant schemes.
Connected through roots, in unity they rise,
A garden of thought, memories in the skies.

Each blossom a story, each petal a voice,
Together they flourish, united by choice.
In the heart of creation, they dance and they play,
Seeds of inspiration, lighting the way.

Harvest the moments, embrace what you sow,
In fields of tomorrow, let your spirit grow.
With patience and courage, let visions expand,
Nurturing futures, together we stand.

The Labyrinth of Thought

Winding through pathways, a maze of the mind,
Each turn a reflection, seeking to find.
Questions like shadows, they linger and tease,
In the depths of silence, they whisper and breeze.

Lost in the corridors, echoes resound,
Searching for answers that seem to confound.
Every dead end leads to new things to see,
Perspectives unfolding, like leaves on a tree.

In labyrinth's heart, a flicker of light,
Hope blooms anew, making darkness take flight.
The journey is winding, yet wisdom will grow,
Navigating obstacles, trusting the flow.

Around each corner, a lesson awaits,
Unraveling secrets, unlocking the gates.
With each new discovery, clarity reigns,
The labyrinth teaches, embracing the pains.

As you weave through, keep faith in your quest,
Learning and growing, you'll find your best.
The labyrinth of thought, a journey so grand,
In its winding embrace, your dreams will expand.

Illuminating the Unseen

In shadows deep where whispers dwell,
A light ignites, a secret spell.
It pierces through the cloaked night sky,
And bids the dreams of lost hopes fly.

A flicker soft, a guiding flame,
Unraveling paths, igniting fame.
The unseen world begins to gleam,
With every step, a new-found dream.

Wisdom waits in silence profound,
In corners where lost voices sound.
To spark a thought, to kindle light,
In realms obscured, we seek the bright.

An artist's touch, a poet's word,
Awakens visions softly stirred.
Through tangled brush and hidden lines,
The unseen shines in gentle signs.

Shed the veil, let colors flow,
Transform the dark with shades that glow.
For in this dance of light and shade,
The unseen truth is gently laid.

Scribes of the Extraordinary

With pen in hand, they trace the sky,
Words that whisper, shout, and fly.
Each stroke a story, vivid, bold,
Of dreams and visions yet untold.

They carve the air with thoughts profound,
In every silence, echoes found.
From parchment depths to virtual reach,
Their voices rise, their wisdom teach.

In every line, a universe,
In every verse, the heart immersed.
Crafting tales of love and strife,
The scribes breathe life into our life.

Extraordinary in their grace,
They capture hope, time, and space.
With ink of courage, they inspire,
To chase the dreams that never tire.

For every page holds infinite charm,
A sacred space, a healing balm.
In words we find the light distill,
In every heart, a visionary thrill.

Guardians of the Muse

In twilight's glow, they softly tread,
With souls ablaze and hearts widespread.
They nurture sparks that beg to bloom,
In secret corners, life resumes.

With brushes poised and voices clear,
They beckon forth what we hold dear.
To breathe new life in stagnant air,
The guardians rise with art to share.

They weave the threads of fate and dreams,
In every color, every theme.
Through tangled paths of joy and pain,
The muse awakens, sings again.

In every stroke, a tale unfolds,
In every note, a heart retold.
They stand sentinel, both fierce and kind,
The guardians of the creative mind.

As shadows stretch and moments blend,
They guide the hearts that seek to mend.
Through echoes soft, they hold the flame,
In every artist's whispered name.

The Odyssey of Creation

From dawn's first light, the journey starts,
With fleeting thoughts, a thousand arts.
In realms unknown, we venture forth,
To craft the dreams that hold us north.

Each stroke of brush, a wave of grace,
In chaos found, we find our place.
With every challenge, a strength revealed,
The odyssey of hope unsealed.

In tapestry of trials, we weave,
The stories told, the hearts believe.
Through labyrinths of doubt and cheer,
Creation blooms while paths draw near.

The sculptor's touch, the writer's muse,
In every choice, we dare to choose.
From memories deep, the visions rise,
An odyssey beneath the skies.

With passion's fire and courage bright,
We chase the dreams that spark the night.
An endless dance of hearts in flight,
The odyssey shines in shared delight.

The Fabric of Vision

In shadows cast by dreams we weave,
Threads of hope that interleave.
A tapestry of colors bright,
Crafting day from the depths of night.

With each stitch, we find our way,
Guided by the light of day.
A vision born from whispered sighs,
Emerging clear beneath the skies.

Every pattern tells a tale,
Of battles won and hearts that fail.
In the fibers, memories flow,
The fabric of vision starts to grow.

We gather strength from stories shared,
Each frayed edge, a sign we cared.
Together in this loom we stand,
Creating beauty, hand in hand.

So let us weave our lives with grace,
Embroider joy, no thread misplaced.
In every fiber, let love remain,
A lasting mark like summer rain.

Navigating the Abstract

In mists of thought, we drift and sway,
Chasing echoes that fade away.
Colors blend in a fleeting glance,
Painting our minds in a wild dance.

Ideas bloom like flowers rare,
Floating softly in the air.
Abstract paths branch and intertwine,
Leading seekers to truths divine.

With every turn, a choice is made,
Shadows flicker, memories fade.
In chaos, clarity will rise,
As stars emerge from murky skies.

We chart our course through skies of grey,
Finding shapes where we cannot stay.
In the labyrinth of thought we roam,
Mapping realms that feel like home.

Together, we'll sail the unknown seas,
Guided by the whispering breeze.
Navigating dreams and fears alike,
In this abstract world, we ignite.

Dance of the Pioneers

With courage high, we take our stand,
Adventurers in a timeless land.
Step by step, we forge and fight,
Chasing horizons bathed in light.

In fields of wild and untamed grace,
We seek the beauty in every place.
Like stars that twinkle in the night,
We shine brighter when in true sight.

With every leap, we leave a mark,
In the echoes of the wild's spark.
Braving storms, we rise anew,
Dreaming dreams both brave and true.

The dance of life, an endless flow,
In every turn, we learn and grow.
Together, hands entwined in fate,
We spin through paths we cultivate.

So let us twirl on this great stage,
Writing history's vibrant page.
The dance of pioneers, bold and clear,
In every heart, we hold the spear.

The Wonderkeepers

In silent whispers, secrets rest,
Guarded dreams we cherish best.
We gather tales from days gone by,
As stars ignite the evening sky.

With gentle hands, we cradle hope,
Helping weary hearts to cope.
In every story, light will swell,
The wonderkeepers guard it well.

Through fog and fear, we light the way,
In darkest nights, we will not sway.
With each heartbeat, magic spins,
Creating worlds where love begins.

In laughter shared and kindness shown,
The seeds of joy are always sown.
We weave the threads of time and space,
As wonderkeepers, we embrace.

So let us cherish every thread,
The tapestry of dreams we've spread.
Together, we will share our light,
As wonderkeepers, shining bright.

Whispers of Innovation

Softly they speak, ideas take flight,
In the silence, dreams ignite.
Whispers weave through the air,
New visions born from a prayer.

Each thought a seed, ready to grow,
In fertile minds, the sparks do glow.
Innovation dances, wild and free,
Creating worlds we long to see.

Time bends under the weight of the bold,
Stories of wonder waiting to unfold.
Hands that sculpt with passion and fire,
Building bridges to take us higher.

In the heart of night, a light remains,
Through struggles faced, the spirit gains.
Whispers echo in the dark,
Lighting paths with their quiet spark.

So let us listen, let us dare,
To follow the whispers floating in air.
For in the shadows of thought we find,
The whispers of innovation, intertwined.

Crafting the Future

With hands that shape and dreams that fly,
We carve the future, reaching high.
Each stroke a promise, each turn a chance,
In the workshop of life, we dance.

Materials of yesterday, planning today,
Breathing life into plans that sway.
Crafting with care, visions anew,
Colossal changes waiting in view.

Time is the canvas, vast and wide,
We paint our hopes, let passions guide.
Every heartbeat, a pulse of creation,
In the core of our shared inspiration.

Together we build, together we rise,
With dreams as our anchors, we touch the skies.
Crafting a world shaped by hands,
Where futures bloom in fertile lands.

So take up your tools, let's make a way,
With heart and soul, come what may.
For in our crafting, the future does gleam,
A tapestry woven from our dream.

Echoes of the Ingenious

In the halls of thought, echoes resound,
Ideas collide, brilliance is found.
Ingenious minds, forever in play,
Reaching for glory in their own way.

Like whispers of genius, they softly emerge,
In flickers of light, they steadily surge.
Thoughts intertwining, a beautiful show,
Where challenges fade and visions grow.

Curiosity drives every quest,
As they chase shadows, never at rest.
Crafted from hope, built on the grind,
In the echoes of change, they refuse to be blind.

Together they forge paths untried,
With nimble fingers, and hearts open wide.
Inventing tomorrow with each daring dream,
In the chambers of thought, they gleam.

So listen closely to those gentle calls,
For echoes of genius can shatter our walls.
A symphony played on the strings of the mind,
Creating a future, brilliantly aligned.

The Palette of Possibility

On a canvas spread out, colors collide,
The palette of dreams, where hopes abide.
Brushes dipped deep in the hues of the soul,
Painting visions that make us whole.

Each stroke a journey, a path we create,
In the realm of potential, we celebrate.
With shades of wonder, we cover the page,
In the art of living, we find our stage.

From deep blue oceans to golden skies,
Every color tells stories, whispers and sighs.
In the tapestry woven, we see our fate,
With every decision, we navigate.

Daring to dream while colors blend,
Creating a portrait that knows no end.
The palette expands, a world anew,
Where possibilities flourish in every hue.

So let us paint a future so bright,
With vibrant strokes that dance in the light.
For in the palette of possibility lies,
A masterpiece waiting, to rise and surprise.

The Whisper of Possibilities

In the quiet dawn, dreams awake,
Soft echoes of hopes, a gentle shake.
Choices flutter like leaves in flight,
Guiding us softly into the light.

Wisps of fate softly entwine,
Every hesitation, a thread divine.
Voices murmur in the still air,
Inviting the bold, the brave, to dare.

Paths not taken, a flicker of chance,
In every heartbeat, a chance to dance.
Life's tapestry woven with care,
Possibilities linger, floating in air.

In the garden of dreams, seeds are sown,
Cultivating futures, each uniquely grown.
Whispers of wonder, gentle and clear,
Embrace the unknown, dissolve every fear.

So let us wander, let us explore,
For in our hearts, lies an open door.
The whisper of hope sings a sweet song,
In possibilities, we all belong.

Tides of Creation

Waves crash softly upon the shore,
Nature's hand painting evermore.
Brush strokes of blue, glimmers of sand,
Crafting beauty, majestic and grand.

The moon pulls strings in the twilight glow,
Emotions rise and fall like the flow.
With every tide, new visions arise,
A canvas of life beneath vast skies.

Colors dance in the morning light,
Whispers of time, tranquil and bright.
Creation's heartbeat, a rhythmic pulse,
In every crevice, the world convulse.

Shadows and light, they play and weave,
Forming stories that dare to believe.
As the tide retreats, new hopes emerge,
In the ebb and flow, creativity surges.

So let us paddle in this vast sea,
With every wave, our spirits set free.
In the tides of creation, we find our way,
Crafting our dreams, come what may.

Canvases of Uncertainty

In the realm of doubt, colors blend,
Each stroke uncertain, yet we transcend.
A palette of fears, hopes intertwined,
Creating a picture, uniquely designed.

The brush of time dances with chance,
Every twist a daunting romance.
Each layer whispers secrets untold,
Unraveling stories, bright and bold.

Shadows loom, but they also teach,
Lessons of life within our reach.
Every flaw a mark of the brave,
In uncertainty’s grasp, we find what we crave.

With every heartbeat, brushes glide,
Painting the unknown, side by side.
The canvas stretches, inviting our muse,
In this dance of chance, we choose to fuse.

Embrace the messy, the raw, the real,
For within uncertainty, we begin to heal.
Canvases bloom with the colors we bring,
In our imperfections, we learn to sing.

Echoes of Greatness

In the depths of silence, legends rise,
Whispers of greatness illuminate the skies.
Their journeys etched in the sands of time,
Stories of courage, dreams that climb.

With every heartbeat, echoes resound,
In valleys of struggle, hope is found.
Heroes' voices, they stir the soul,
Guiding us gently toward our goal.

In echoes of laughter, joy abound,
Moments of triumph, their magic profound.
Through trials faced, we find our song,
In the tapestry of life, we all belong.

So let us rise, let our spirits soar,
In the wake of the echoes, we’ll seek for more.
Greatness is born from the flames of pain,
In unity’s embrace, we thrive again.

With every marker laid on our path,
We chase the sunlight, defying wrath.
In the echoes of greatness, our dreams ignite,
Together, we stand, ready to fight.

The Forge of New Realities

In shadows cast by hopes unmade,
We shape the dreams that we parade.
With sparks of thought, we light the fire,
Creating worlds that never tire.

Each hammer's strike, a vision clear,
As molten dreams begin to sear.
With every breath, a tale unfolds,
In forges warm, the new holds gold.

The anvil's song, a call to rise,
To break the chains, to touch the skies.
In every forge, a heart ignites,
Crafting futures in endless nights.

A dance of flames, a sculptor's hand,
With passion pure, we make our stand.
Reality bends, the old gives way,
To forge anew, to shape the day.

So gather round, the brave, the bold,
In unity, our stories told.
With every spark, a new embrace,
In the forge of dreams, find your place.

Navigators of the Imagination

We sail the seas where thoughts collide,
With winds of change, we take the ride.
The stars above, our guiding light,
Navigators bold in the night.

Uncharted realms await our gaze,
In currents strong, we weave our ways.
With maps of dreams, we chart the course,
In every heart, a hidden force.

The waves of doubt, we learn to tame,
In every storm, we call our name.
Through tempest's roar, we hear the sound,
Of visions vast that know no bound.

With trepidation, we dive deep,
Into the depths where secrets sleep.
Our vessels strong, our spirits bright,
Navigators of day and night.

Together we explore and find,
The endless treasures of the mind.
With courage fierce, we chase the dawn,
As navigators, we're never gone.

Voyagers of the Mind

With every thought, we take our flight,
As voyagers lost in endless night.
Through realms of wonder, over waves,
We seek the truth, the heart enslaves.

A compass forged from dreams we see,
Guides us through depths of mystery.
In silence thick, we hear the call,
Of places where the shadows fall.

With each new thought, we build a bridge,
Connecting worlds where minds can fridge.
In every nook, a spark ignites,
With whispers soft, the dark ignites.

We journey far, through time and space,
With open hearts, we seek the grace.
Together bound, we venture deep,
As voyagers, our dreams we keep.

So let us roam, let spirits soar,
In lands of thought, forevermore.
With every step, a story finds,
The endless path of curious minds.

Bridging the Unfathomable

In echoes soft, we seek the way,
To bridge the gaps where shadows play.
With threads of light, we weave the night,
Connecting realms with endless might.

Where silence dwells, there dreams arise,
A tapestry beneath the skies.
In whispered hopes, we find our song,
As bridges form, we all belong.

With hands outstretched, we break the mold,
In unity, our tales unfold.
No distance great, no chasm wide,
Can dim the spark we hold inside.

Through fears unknown, we boldly stride,
With open hearts, we turn the tide.
In every thread, a bond is spun,
Bridging worlds where light has won.

Together we create the space,
For dreams to flourish, fears erase.
With courage fierce, we face the call,
Bridging the unfathomable for all.

The Symphony of Voices

In twilight's gentle embrace, they sing,
Whispers of dreams on the wind do cling.
Each tone a story, woven in air,
Harmonies rise, dispelling despair.

A chorus of heartbeats, souls intertwine,
Through laughter and sorrow, together we shine.
Echoes of moments, both bitter and sweet,
In the concert of life, our voices repeat.

From shadows we gather, united and bold,
Crafting our journey, a tale to be told.
The symphony dances, a vibrant display,
Each note a reminder that night turns to day.

In pauses we listen, in silence we find,
The depth of connection that flows through mankind.
Every voice matters, a crucial part played,
In the grand orchestration, no one is weighed.

So let us not falter, but rise and rejoice,
In the beautiful chorus, we all have a voice.
Through laughter and tears, we seal our pact tight,
Together we flourish, through darkness to light.

Journeys Through the Unknown

Beneath the vast sky, we wander and roam,
With footprints in sand, we make the world home.
Each horizon a beckon, a call to explore,
In the depths of the wild, we find so much more.

Across verdant valleys and mountains so high,
With stars as our compass, we learn how to fly.
Every step a story, each moment a chance,
In the tapestry woven, we learn how to dance.

Through rivers and forests, where shadows play tricks,
In the heart of the journey, we find the right mix.
With courage as armor, we face the unknown,
In the whispers of nature, our truth is shown.

Together with strangers, we forge bonds anew,
Sharing laughter and lessons, as friendships accrue.
In the map of our hearts, we navigate fate,
Embracing the unknown, it's never too late.

So let us embark on this journey so grand,
With hope as our guide, united we stand.
For in every adventure, a part of us grows,
Through journeys unknown, our spirit knows.

The Light of Insight

In the stillness of thought, clarity blooms,
Illuminating shadows, dispelling the glooms.
With each flicker of reason, the mind starts to soar,
Glimmers of wisdom, opening doors.

In moments of quiet, the answers reveal,
A tapestry woven with fibers of feel.
Through questions and ponder, new pathways unfold,
The light of insight, a treasure to hold.

As dawn breaks the silence, igniting the sky,
Perception expands, inviting us to try.
With courage, we venture to embrace the unknown,
In the garden of thought, our seeds are sown.

In dialogues lingering, ideas collide,
Through sharing and learning, we turn the tide.
With insight as lantern, we traverse the maze,
Illuminating truths in life's vibrant haze.

So cherish each moment, and let wisdom flow,
For in every lesson, our spirits will grow.
In the light of insight, we find our true place,
As we navigate life with unyielding grace.

Sculpting the Abstract

With strokes of the mind, concepts take shape,
In the hands of the dreamer, the formless escape.
Through shadows and colors, a vision is born,
Crafting the essence, where ideas are worn.

In the canvas of thought, imagination soars,
Molding the abstract, opening doors.
With each gentle touch, dimensions unveil,
A symphony sculpted, where senses can sail.

In the realm of creation, the boundaries blur,
With whispers of meaning, our passions confer.
Through turmoil and silence, we shape what we seek,
In the dance of expression, the heart finds its beat.

So gather the fragments, the scattered remaining,
In the beauty of chaos, we find the explaining.
As visions converge into stories refined,
In sculpting the abstract, our essence aligned.

With passion as chisel, and dreams as our guide,
We carve out existence, with nowhere to hide.
For in every creation, our truth takes its flight,
In the art of the abstract, we discover the light.

Bridging the Divide

Two worlds stand apart, yet reach,
Hope flows in whispers, words we teach.
Hands grasping tight, hearts open wide,
Together we'll stand, no need to hide.

In shadows we walk, fear and doubt,
But kindness can flicker, like a shout.
Brick by brick we will build our way,
Through laughter and love, brightening the day.

The rivers may swirl, they may roar,
But bridges of trust can build evermore.
With every step, the path will unfold,
Stories of courage, together retold.

Differences fade, as we share our sights,
Found in the echoes of shared delights.
An endless horizon, as we pave,
A future united, the bold, the brave.

So let us embark, through heart's loyal guide,
Together in friendship, forever allied.
Across the divide, we stretch our embrace,
In unity's dance, we find our place.

Step into the Vision

Dreamers arise, take your stand,
With hope in your heart and light in hand.
Envision the change, feel the spark,
Together we'll brighten the world from dark.

A canvas awaits, colors abound,
Brush strokes of passion, let them resound.
Each moment a chance to create anew,
Step into the vision, let it guide you through.

The road may be winding, the mountains steep,
But visions are treasures, promises we keep.
With every heartbeat, we breathe in the dream,
Flowing like rivers, bright as a beam.

With heads held high, we'll face the storm,
In unity's safety, we all transform.
The vision is clear, a future we chase,
Step into the light, find your place.

So gather your courage, take that first leap,
Plant seeds of hope, in hearts they'll seep.
Together we'll shine, like stars in the night,
Step into the vision, embrace the light.

Seasons of Imagination

In springtime blooms, possibilities rise,
With laughter and dreams that fill the skies.
A canvas of colors, fresh and new,
In each gentle breeze, inspiration grew.

Summer's warm embrace, full of cheer,
Where whispers of magic draw us near.
In fields of wonder, we dance and play,
Imagination blooms in a vibrant array.

Autumn leaves fall, a tapestry bright,
Stories unfold in the golden light.
Each crackling moment, a memory made,
In this season of change, fears start to fade.

Winter descends with a quiet grace,
In blankets of snow, dreams find their space.
In the hush of the world, we pause and reflect,
Imagination within, we gently protect.

Through seasons we roam, hearts open wide,
In the garden of thoughts, let love be our guide.
Each moment a treasure, a story to spin,
In the seasons of life, let the magic begin.

The Flare of Inspiration

A flicker ignites, a spark in the night,
With passion as fuel, it flares up bright.
Ideas like flames dance and soar,
In the heart of creation, we yearn for more.

From whispers of dreams to bold cries of art,
Each stroke on the canvas, a piece of the heart.
Inspiration flows like a river so wide,
Carving through mountains, nothing to hide.

In moments of doubt, let the embers glow,
For within us all, the fire will show.
Through shadows and trials, we gather our might,
The flare of inspiration, our guiding light.

With courage as armor, we chase and explore,
The wonders that wait, always offering more.
In the blaze of the mind, possibilities sing,
Fueling the passion, the joy that it brings.

So let the flames burn, let imagination fly,
Through the depths of our souls, reaching high.
A journey of creation, together we'll share,
The flare of inspiration is always there.

Sparks of Innovation

In the silence of night, ideas ignite,
Flickering bits of brilliance take flight.
Dreamers gather, visions unfold,
Whispers of futures, bright and bold.

Machines hum with a rhythmic tune,
Crafting wonders beneath the moon.
Hands to nurture, minds collide,
In the furnace of thought, passions abide.

Blueprints dance on parchment bare,
Each stroke a promise, each line a dare.
The pulse of progress, a steady beat,
Innovation's rhythm, strong and sweet.

Eager hearts with fire within,
Launch forth the dreams, let the quest begin.
From here to there, we pave the way,
Sparks of innovation guide our play.

United we stand, no fear of change,
In the vibrant chaos, we rearrange.
Together we soar, ideas unfurl,
As we light up the world, a new pearl.

The Canvas of Tomorrow

Brush strokes painting a new dawn's light,
Imaginations flourish, taking flight.
Colors blend in a vivid embrace,
The canvas breathes, a boundless space.

Dreamers gather, visions align,
Crafting a future that's truly divine.
Hues of hope in every swirl,
A masterpiece born, our dreams unfurl.

With every stroke, a story is told,
Of brave hearts and spirits, fearless and bold.
We sketch the pathways to realms unknown,
In this vibrant garden, our seeds are sown.

From the depths of night to the break of day,
The canvas invites us to dance and play.
Together we paint, across the expanse,
In the palette of life, we take our chance.

The colors of tomorrow, bright and clear,
Each brush stroke echoing our dreams sincere.
As the sunlight glistens, visions ignite,
On the canvas of tomorrow, we unite.

Luminaries in the Shadows

In the dimmest corners, light breaks through,
Soft glimmers dance, as if they knew.
Whispers of hope in muted tones,
Illuminating paths where courage hones.

Stars emerge from the thick of night,
Casting their magic, a gentle light.
Guiding lost souls back to the way,
In the shadows, they find their play.

Echoes of laughter, whispers of dreams,
A symphony played through muted beams.
Beneath the surface, the magic flows,
Where luminaries gather, heartbeats glow.

With every spark, the shadows bend,
Creating a world where love transcends.
Together we rise, against the tide,
For in the dark, our hopes reside.

Through the veil of night, we shall sing,
For every shadow, a light will bring.
In unity, we stand, proud and true,
As luminaries guiding, me and you.

Crafting Tomorrow's Legends

With hands steady, we carve the stone,
Molding the future from dreams we've grown.
Each legend born from a spark of desire,
Fueled by the visions that never tire.

They rise from the ashes, heroes of heart,
In the canvas of time, they play their part.
Stories entwined, through laughter and strife,
Each breath they take, a new lease on life.

In the echo of time, their voices remain,
Tales of courage, woven through pain.
With every legend, a lesson to learn,
In the flames of history, our passions burn.

Together we build on the shoulders of giants,
Creating a future where spirit defies it.
In every heartbeat, rich and profound,
The spirit of legends in whispers resound.

Crafting tomorrow, with each woven thread,
In the tapestry of life, where dreams are bred.
We write our story, unyielding, proud,
Crafting tomorrow's legends, we sing out loud.

The Quest for the Unique

In a world with faces bright,
I seek a spark, a guiding light.
Through the shadows, whispers call,
To embrace the rise and fall.

Each path I tread, a tale unfolds,
With every step, courage molds.
In the signs that fortune sends,
My heart believes, the journey bends.

From valleys low to mountains tall,
I chase the rare, answering the call.
The treasure lies within the quest,
For what is unique, I know is best.

Through tangled woods and rivers wide,
I wander forth, with hope as guide.
In every glance, in every sound,
The unique spark can always be found.

In twilight's hue, I stand alone,
The whispers guide, my heart has grown.
Finding gems in life's embrace,
The quest for the unique I chase.

Harmonies of the Unseen

In the silence, music swells,
Whispers soft, where magic dwells.
Notes entwined in gentle breeze,
Creating worlds that aim to please.

Colors dance in darkest night,
Painting dreams with softest light.
Hidden rhythms fill the air,
An unseen chant, serenely fair.

In each heartbeat, echoes play,
Guiding souls along the way.
Through shadows deep, and fears that cling,
The harmonies of life do sing.

Moments shared, a bond we weave,
In the unseen, we truly believe.
Chasing whispers, soft and clear,
In each note, we hold what's dear.

With every glance, with every sigh,
The unseen love that could not die.
Together, we explore the grace,
In harmonies, we find our place.

Mirrors of the Soul

In the stillness, reflections break,
Glimmers of dreams our hearts awake.
Eyes that shine, revealing truth,
Every glance uncovers youth.

With every word, a story told,
Mirrors grasp each child and old.
Tales of laughter, tales of pain,
In the mirror, we find our gain.

Shattered pieces, mended whole,
In the depth, we see the soul.
Honesty in every gaze,
In reflections, we find our maze.

Seeking wisdom, seeking grace,
Mirrors bring a warm embrace.
Through darkened paths, through brightened skies,
In the soul, the truth never lies.

Each moment captured, time stands still,
In the mirror's light, hearts can fill.
Embrace the shadow, embrace the light,
For in the soul, all is bright.

Dreamers in the Spectrum

Beneath the sky, in colors grand,
Dreamers gather, hand in hand.
Across the spectrum, visions flow,
With every heartbeat, dreams do grow.

In rainbows bright, hopes intertwine,
Mapping futures, yours and mine.
Each color shines, a beacon clear,
In this spectrum, we draw near.

From dusk till dawn, the dreams take flight,
Casting shadows, embracing light.
With open hearts and open eyes,
The spectrum whispers, it never lies.

In every brushstroke, stories find,
The dance of dreams, with love entwined.
In vibrant hues, our spirits soar,
Dreamers unite, forevermore.

The world awaits, let colors sing,
Together we can create a spring.
In dreams that burst, like stars above,
We find our path, we find our love.

Milton Keynes UK
Ingram Content Group UK Ltd.
UKHW021235310824
447642UK00006B/236

9 789916 8